CULTURE IN ACTION

Contortionists and Cannons

An Acrobatic Look at the Circus

Marc Tyler Nobleman

Chicago, Illinois

www.heinemannraintree.com
Visit our website to find out more information about Heinemann-Raintree books.

To order:

☎ Phone 888-454-2279

🖥 Visit www.heinemannraintree.com to browse our catalog and order online.

Edited by Louise Galpine, Megan Cotugno, and Abby Colich
Designed by Ryan Frieson
Original illustrations ©Capstone Global Library, Ltd.
Illustrated by Cavedweller Studio, Randy Schirz
Picture research by Liz Alexander
Originated by Capstone Global Library, Ltd.
Printed and bound in China by China Translation & Printing Services, Ltd.

13 12 11 10
10 9 8 7 6 5 4 3 2 1

Library of Congress Cataloging-in-Publication Data
Nobleman, Marc Tyler.
  Contortionists and cannons : an acrobatic look at the circus / Marc Tyler Nobleman.
    p. cm. -- (Culture in action)
  Includes bibliographical references and index.
  ISBN 978-1-4109-3919-7 (hc)
  1. Circus--Juvenile literature. [1. Circus.] I. Title.
  GV1817.N63 2010
  791.3--dc22
                        2009050697

Acknowledgments

The author and publishers are grateful to the following for permission to reproduce copyright material:

We would like to thank the following for permission to reproduce photographs: Alamy pp. 4 (© Ambient Images Inc.), 6 (© North Wind Picture Archives); Corbis pp. 7 (© Historical Picture Archive), 12 (© Swim Ink 2, LLC), 19 (© Nicole Duplaix), 21 (© Bettmann), 22 (© Ursula Dueren/epa), 25 (© Lowell Georgia), 26 (© Christinne Muschi/Reuters); Getty Images pp. 10, 11, 29 (Hulton Archive), 13 (AFP), 14 (Jupiterimages/Workbook Stock), 18 (Scott Wintrow); iStockphoto p. 5 (© Peter Engelsted Jonasen); Courtesy of the Board of Trustees, National Gallery of Art, Washington p. 8 (John Bill Ricketts by Gilbert Stuart, Gift of Mrs. Robert B. Noyes in memory of Elisa Riggs, Image Courtesy of the Board of Trustees, National Gallery of Art, Washington); Photolibrary p. 9 (The National Archives/Imagestate); Rex Features p. 28 (SNAP); Shutterstock pp. 16 (© Tatiana Morozova), 24 (© PavleMarjanovic).

Cover photograph of an acrobat of Balagan from Las Vegas, USA performing a flying aerial chiffon on stage during the World Acrobats Show, 2009 in Bangkok reproduced with permission of Corbis (© Narong Sangnak/epa).

We would like to thank Sylvia Hernandez-DiStasi and Jackie Murphy for their invaluable help in the preparation of this book.

Every effort has been made to contact copyright holders of any material reproduced in this book. Any omissions will be rectified in subsequent printings if notice is given to the publisher.

All the Internet addresses (URLs) given in this book were valid at the time of going to press. However, due to the dynamic nature of the Internet, some addresses may have changed, or sites may have changed or ceased to exist since publication. While the author and Publishers regret any inconvenience this may cause readers, no responsibility for any such changes can be accepted by either the author or the Publishers.

Author
Marc Nobleman is the author of more than 70 books. He speaks regularly to young people about the joys, challenges, and methods of writing books.

Literacy consultant
Jackie Murphy is Director of Arts at the Center of Teaching and Learning, Northeastern Illinois University. She works with teachers, artists, and school leaders internationally.

Expert
Sylvia Hernandez-DiStasi began performing at the age of seven with her family of acrobats, The Hernandez Troupe. She currently runs The Actors Gymnasium, a circus and performing arts school.

Contents

Some words are printed in bold, **like this**. You can find out what they mean by looking in the glossary on page 30.

Step Right Up!

Outside a town, an enormous, colorful tent stands in a field. Inside are treats for children of all ages. See fierce animals and fearless **acrobats**! Smell sawdust and sweet cotton candy! Hear peppy music! Feel your sides ache from laughing at lovable clowns! The circus is here!

What is a circus?

A circus is a **troupe** (group) of people and sometimes animals that performs dazzling entertainments for an audience. In various forms, circuses have been entertaining people worldwide since ancient Rome. Today, some circuses blend traditions from around the world.

The word *circus* comes from the Latin word for *circle*. At first, circuses took place in a single circular area called a **ring**. To draw bigger crowds, circus owners added more **acts**, or performances. To fit those acts, they added additional rings. The three-ring circus became especially popular. Some circuses have as many as five rings.

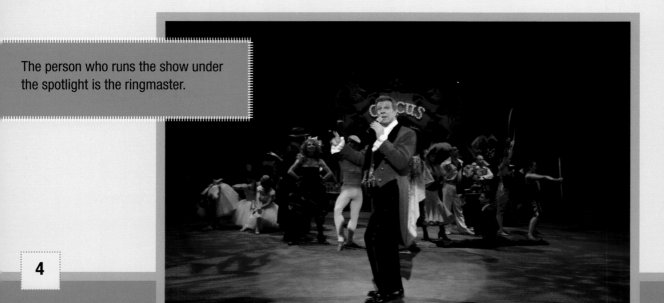

The person who runs the show under the spotlight is the ringmaster.

Circuses in Europe did not begin using tents when American circuses did. They continued to put on shows in permanent structures.

Different town each day

Traditional circuses traveled from village to village. Because they were performing outdoors or in simple structures, they took the winter off.

A circus would set up at dawn, use a parade in the morning to draw a crowd, perform one or two shows, pack up after dark, and move to the next town overnight. Today some circuses stay in one permanent location.

For hundreds of years, for thousands of people, the most exciting day of the year has been when the circus comes to town.

Circus travel

Early circuses traveled by wagons. In the 1800s, many began to use trains. In the 1900s, some circuses switched to trucks.

This illustration shows chariots racing in the Circus Maximus in ancient Rome.

The Circus Through the Centuries

Circuses date back at least as far as ancient Rome. The first and biggest circus in ancient Rome began around 50 BCE in the Circus Maximus, an enormous stadium. **Spectators** were thrilled by events such as chariot races, **equestrian** (horse) **acts**, **acrobatics**, and wild-animal displays.

After the Roman Empire ended, hundreds of years passed before the term *circus* was commonly used again. However, people did continue to enjoy circus-type entertainment. In the Middle Ages, the period from roughly 500 to 1500 CE, **acrobats** and animal trainers traveled throughout Europe performing at fairs and markets.

Birth of the modern circus

A British former soldier named Philip Astley is often considered the father of the modern circus. In 1768 he began performing horse-riding stunts in London. In one of his tricks, he stood on a galloping horse with one foot on the horse's back and the other on the horse's head. Astley had figured out that riding around a **ring** of a certain size helped him keep his balance. He called this ring "the Circle." Performing in a ring became a circus tradition.

Astley called his performance ring "the Circle." Performing in a ring became a circus tradition.

Soon Astley added musicians and a clown called Mr. Merryman to his performances. He also built Astley's Amphitheatre, a large, permanent hall in which to perform. Astley did not describe his show as a "circus." However, his nearby competitor, Charles Hughes, used the term for his own show, and it stuck.

The circus spreads

In 1782 Astley opened a second circus in Paris. He went on to found a total of 19 circuses across Europe. Hughes brought his act to Russia.

The circus in North America

Inspired by Astley and Hughes, a talented rider named John Bill Ricketts brought the circus to North America. His first U.S. performance was in Philadelphia in 1793. It took place in an open-air structure that seated 800 spectators— and which Ricketts built himself. It was a hit. Before Ricketts's circus was a month old, President George Washington attended a performance.

Like Astley and Hughes, Ricketts started with equestrian acts and later added acrobatics and comedy. Ricketts also toured his show along the eastern United States and Canada.

Growth of the circus

As circuses became popular, they developed different traditions. Traveling circuses usually performed in uncovered wooden structures. In Delaware in 1825, Joshuah Purdy Brown held his show under a large canvas tent.

John Bill Ricketts brought the circus to North America.

A tent meant the show could go on even in the rain. Also, tents were portable. Circuses no longer had to buy wood and build structures at each new site. Tents also allowed circuses to move faster. They could now perform in more cities—and make more money.

This poster **advertises** the circus at the 1886 World's Fair.

Menageries

People had displayed exotic animals, including lions and polar bears, in North America by the middle of the 1700s. In 1832 Brown became the first person to add a **menagerie**, or a group of animals, to a circus.

Star elephants

The first elephant in North America arrived in 1796 and later joined a circus. The second elephant in North America was named Old Bet. In the early 1800s, her owner charged people money to see her. He walked her from town to town at night so fewer people would get a glimpse for free.

The Greatest Shows on Earth

In the 1840s businessman P. T. Barnum became famous for running a museum of "**curiosities**" in New York City. He was brilliant at drawing a crowd with rare **attractions** such as General Tom Thumb, a dwarf who sang, danced, and imitated famous people. Barnum also made up attractions such as a "mermaid mummy." The mummy was actually a dummy made from a monkey and a fish.

In 1871 Barnum and businessman W. C. Coup formed a circus that would also display Barnum's curiosities. The curiosities developed into a popular circus feature called a **sideshow**, which is a smaller attraction at a circus. They **advertised** their circus as "the Greatest Show on Earth."

In 1880 Barnum partnered with circus organizer James Bailey. They created a three-**ring extravaganza** that became known as the Barnum and Bailey Circus.

General Tom Thumb was a small man with big talent. He could sing, dance, and imitate famous people.

A talented family

Meanwhile, in Wisconsin, five brothers named Ringling had grown up in awe of the circus. In 1884 they created their own. Each brother had a skill. One was good at advertising. Another was good at picking **acts**. Another handled the money. Together they were a success.

In 1919, by which time Barnum, Bailey, and more than half of the Ringling brothers had died, their circuses merged to become the Ringling Bros. and Barnum & Bailey Circus. It is still one of the biggest names in circuses today.

The circus goes wild

Beginning in the 1880s, William "Buffalo Bill" Cody toured a cowboy-**themed** circus called Buffalo Bill's Wild West. Acts included rodeo stunts, shooting competitions, and short plays about train robberies and bison hunting.

This poster advertises the combined show of P. T. Barnum and James Bailey.

Thrilling Acts

At the circus, audiences are often looking up. **Acrobats**, tight-rope walkers, and human cannonballs entertain audiences from above. While watching **aerial** (in the air) displays, some **spectators** "ooh" and "aah." Others hold their breath. Everyone hopes no one falls.

Air acrobats

Trapeze artists perform in multiple ways. In static (not moving) trapeze, performers balance on and hang from trapezes (bars hung between two ropes) that stay in place. Swinging trapeze artists perform on moving trapezes. In flying trapeze, the flyer leaps from one trapeze and grabs another trapeze or a catcher on another trapeze. Flying **aerialists** work over a safety net.

VAN AMBURGH & CO'S

CANTON MAY 17
MENAGERIE, CIRCUS AND COLOSSEUM

In the earliest trapeze **acts**, performers leaped to and from bars connected to the ground.

Daring young man

In 1859 French aerialist Jules Léotard became the first known person to do a midair somersault while performing a flying trapeze act. He wore a skintight costume that is now named after him.

Top of the big top

About 9 meters (30 feet) up, circus tightrope walkers cross a wire thinner than 2.5 centimeters (1 inch). Some carry a pole to help balance. On the wire, tightrope walkers do more than walk. Additional stunts include juggling and forming human pyramids. Some perform without a net. This makes the audience feel the act is more dangerous.

Hanging by a thread

In *corde lisse* (French for "smooth rope"), an aerialist performs various hangs and other tricks on a **vertical** (up and down) rope. A similar act is the "Spanish web," in which aerialists also spin on the rope. Both acts require strength and grace.

This trapeze artist is wearing a safety wire in case she falls.

Boom!

Cannon acts offer thrills that are both high and fast. A person shot out of a cannon can travel 105 kilometers (65 miles) an hour.

13

Unbelievable feats

Not all the circus thrills are on high. Amazing stunts also fill the **rings** below. Many acts wow spectators at the ground.

"Strongmen" and "strongwomen" were popular circus **attractions** in the 1800s. They bent metal bars in their hands and lifted heavy blocks of metal.

Contortionists bend their bodies into positions that do not seem humanly possible. Because of their training and flexibility, it is not painful, although it may look that way.

Stilt walkers balance high in the air as they walk on high poles, or stilts.

Sword swallowers do not eat swords. They slide them far down their throat. It takes practice and concentration, but it remains highly risky.

Fire breathers appear to shoot flames from their mouth. By spitting fuel such as kerosene over a flame in certain ways, they create fiery effects.

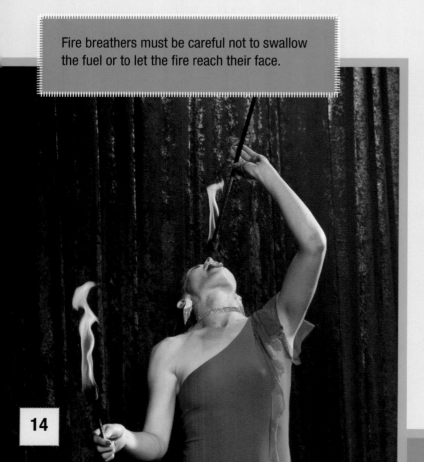

Fire breathers must be careful not to swallow the fuel or to let the fire reach their face.

Spin plates

Many circus skills would be fun to learn, but let's start with one that does not require a net!

Plate spinners spin plates atop vertical sticks. The sticks are held or lined up in front of the performers. The performers must keep all the plates spinning at once.

Steps to follow:

1. Find a straight stick or other wooden bar that is .05 or 1 meter (2 or 3 feet) long.

2. Get a heavy-duty paper or plastic plate.

3. In a clear area outside, place the plate on top of the stick and try to spin it.

4. Experiment with different methods. Should you keep your legs straight or bend them at the knees? Where should you look while you spin? Practice with a sibling or friend.

5. When you are both ready, compete to see who can keep a plate spinning longer.

Practice plate-spinning before you compete with your friends to see who can spin the longest.

Circus Favorites

People go to the circus to gasp, but also to laugh. The **comic relief** of a circus is the clowns. Many clowns do not speak during performances. Certain clown routines have become classics, such as the small car that somehow holds many clowns.

Clown categories

There are several kinds of clowns. "Whiteface clowns" commonly wear white makeup and small, pointed hats. Their clothes can be either baggy or fitted and usually match. When performing with other clowns, a whiteface clown often plays the "boss."

"Auguste clowns" commonly wear bright wigs, mismatched clothes, and floppy shoes. Their faces often feature big red noses and outlined mouths. Much of their humor is **slapstick**, such as falling and chasing.

"Character clowns" come in different varieties, such as the tramp or the police officer. They often perform alone.

Some clowns do more than make an audience laugh. This auguste clown performs **acrobatics** as well.

Some modern clowns do not wear wild makeup or costumes. They sometimes interact with the audience, even asking for volunteers.

Design a clown costume

Create a new, modern clown look for the 2010s.

Steps to follow:

1. Look at pictures of existing clown types online or in books. Look at the range of different costumes and makeup. Make a mental note of what you like and do not like about each.

2. Choose an idea for your clown. Do you want him to be punk, formal, tropical, robotic, or something else?

3. Sketch two designs based on your idea. You may use elements from existing clowns, but most of your design should be new. Think about clothing, makeup design, and what will be funny!

4. Decide which of your designs you like better. Ink and color that design.

5. Name your new type of clown. Display your new clown for friends and family to see.

What will your new clown look like? Will any of its features remind you of yourself.

Circuses save the biggest animal acts for last. Elephants often perform after the big cats.

Circus critters

Some of the most popular circus stars are furry and four-legged. Animals including horses, elephants, lions, and bears have appeared in circuses. Some animal **acts** perform in an unexpected way. For example, elephants stand on their hind legs and walk in a row. Other animal acts impress audiences because of the danger involved. Trainers have walked into the cages of growling big cats.

Celebrity circus creatures

Two of the biggest stars in circus history were big themselves. In 1882 Barnum introduced Jumbo, a 6.4-tonne (7.0-ton), 3.7-meter- (12-foot-) tall elephant. As a **publicity** stunt, Barnum had Jumbo lead an elephant parade across the Brooklyn Bridge. Now the word *jumbo* means "enormous."

Debuting in 1938, Gargantua (as in gargantuan, meaning "large") was a gorilla with a scarred face. His frightening look made him popular, and his popularity saved the Ringling Brothers circus from going out of business.

Against their will

While the use of animals in circuses is a beloved tradition, it also causes concern. Some people claim that the training is abusive, and that the animals perform out of fear. Investigators have seen trainers strike elephants with whips and hooks. Some stunts put animals in danger, such as when a tiger jumps through a fire hoop. But circuses and trainers claim animals are treated with love and are well-cared for. Animal rights organizations are working to free circus animals. Some countries ban animals from circuses, and some circuses choose to have no animals.

Flea circus

In the 1800s and 1900s, flea circuses were popular **sideshow attractions**. Real fleas were attached to tiny bicycles or chariots. **Spectators** looked through special lenses to watch the fleas "perform." A flea circus has a limited audience—only the number of people who can crowd around a small table. To earn more money, flea circus managers would run dozens of 10-minute shows a day.

Two fleas attached to carts race during this miniature circus.

The Dark Side of Circuses

Circuses bring great joy, but they have also been places of cruelty and tragedy. Many circuses have taken advantage of people who are different from others. Other times, tragedy has struck during circuses.

The shame of circuses past

Some circuses used to include "freak shows." They featured people with unusual talents, such as sword swallowers, and those who looked different, such as people with many tattoos. They also included people who looked different but not by choice, such as bearded women and so-called "Siamese twins," or conjoined (attached) twins. Some of these people were forced to appear in freak shows, but others wanted to join.

Throughout the 1900s, more and more people felt that freak shows unkindly took advantage of some people. Circuses stopped including freak shows. Now it is no longer acceptable to display a person as a "freak."

The Connecticut fire

On July 6, 1944, disaster struck a circus in Hartford, Connecticut. To stop a leak in the tent, the circus had waterproofed it. Tragically, they used substances that burn easily, including gasoline.

Twenty minutes into the show, the tent caught fire. The band began to play "Stars and Stripes Forever." At the circus, that song is played only during emergencies. It alerts the performers that there is danger and is meant to calm the audience as they exit. Yet that day, the music did not help.

Spectators run for their lives during the Hartford circus fire of 1944.

Almost 7,000 **spectators** were in attendance. Some did not realize they could have escaped under the tent flaps. Instead they rushed to where they had entered, but animal equipment now blocked the way. The tent burned to ashes in six minutes. Hundreds were injured, and 168 people died.

A sad statistic

In terms of lives lost, the Hartford fire was the worst circus disaster in history.

Learning Circus Skills

Today, anybody—both kids and adults—can learn how to participate in a circus. They go to circus schools or camps for young people.

Circus schools

Special schools worldwide teach circus skills. Ringling Bros. and Barnum & Bailey Clown College, located in Florida and Wisconsin, taught professional clowning from 1968 to 1997, and now teaches clowns all over the country. **Trapeze** schools in cities including New York City and London give everyday people the chance to feel the rush of an **aerial act**.

Children **acrobats** perform on a trapeze at this circus in Munich, Germany.

Through the Mobile Mini Circus for Children in Afghanistan, kids create and perform their own circus. In Australia an organization called Cirkidz trains people as young as two-and-a-half in the circus arts.

Youth circuses and camps

Circus Smirkus is an international youth circus and camp based in Vermont. Its performers are between 10 and 18 years old. Every summer it introduces a new story line and goes on tour, doing 70 shows in two months. Circus camps can also be found in countries including the United Kingdom and Germany.

Write circus lyrics

"Thunder and Blazes", composed by Louis-Philippe Laurendeau, based on "Entrance of the Gladiators" by Julius Fucík is a famous circus march. But it had no words to sing along to...until now.

Steps to follow:

1. Listen to "Thunder and Blazes" online or on a CD. (You will recognize it!) How does the music make you feel?

2. Think of how the music reminds you of the circus. Does it remind you of acrobats, animals, or something else from the circus? Write lyrics (words) to fit the music. Make the words describe a circus adventure!

3. Perform your new mix for family and friends. If you do not want to sing alone, first teach it to a sibling or friend.

When writing lyrics to "Thunder and Blazes," think about how the music makes you feel.

23

Reinventing the Circus

Two hundred years ago, a circus was often a town's only entertainment for the whole year. Today, circuses compete every day against movies, concerts, theater, sports, games, reading, television, and the Internet for people's time and money.

An international feel

While circuses still entertain with upbeat music, clueless clowns, and spine-tingling **acts**, they have updated these features for modern audiences. Many circuses today bring in performers, acts, and customs from around the world.

Telling a story

Circuses used to be a series of unrelated acts. Today some circuses tell a story and have a **theme**, or central idea. In some recent circuses, there are no animal performers. The music is new and created specifically for that circus. The performance is in a theater, not a tent. Some use modern machines such as motorcycles. This style of circus is called "*cirque nouveau*," which is French for "new circus."

Members of the Great Chinese Circus perform during their tour throughout Europe.

This motorcyclist rides around the inside of a metal cage as a part of a circus.

Traditional circuses keep up

In response to successful new circuses, the long-running Ringling Bros. and Barnum & Bailey Circus tried a new kind of show in 2006. It was the first major change the circus had made in 50 years.

The three **rings** and big cats were gone, but the circus added a running story about a present-day family that dreams of joining the circus. It also added a jumbo video screen to show story flashbacks and instant replays.

Biggest big top

As of 2009 the largest permanent big top in the world is at Circus Circus, a hotel in Las Vegas, Nevada. In 1997 it changed from being traditional to being a more modern kind of circus.

Circus Oz

Circus Oz premiered in Australia in 1978 and has since performed in dozens of countries. Some circuses have a large cast, but each Circus Oz show features only 11 to 13 performers. Each performer has multiple skills, from **acrobatics** to clowning. Circus Oz uses a wide range of elements, including rock and roll and humor.

In the Cirque du Soleil production of *Ovo*, the performers play insects who discover a strange egg.

Cirque du Soleil

Founded in Québec, Canada, Cirque du Soleil (meaning "Circus of the Sun" in French) began in 1984. This circus company produces multiple shows at once, each with its own theme. Some shows stay in one location, while others tour the world.

Cirque du Soleil's experiments go beyond new stories and music. One Cirque du Soleil show, *O*, features underwater acrobatics performed in a giant tank. Another show, *KÀ*, doesn't use a traditional stage. Instead the action takes place on large, movable platforms.

Circus Amok

In New York City parks, Circus Amok puts on free circuses with jugglers, **stilt** walkers, and life-sized puppets. Founded by bearded woman Jennifer Miller, Circus Amok's message is the importance of being true to yourself and fair to others.

"Dark" circuses

Some new circuses combine circus **acts** with street performance, comedy, and electronic music. Other groups feature comedy and rap music to appeal to younger audiences. Modern circuses can also have a creepy side to them, unlike traditional circuses.

Familiar faces

Some circuses include characters created in other types of entertainment. For example, the Cole Bros. Circus has featured acts with Spider-Man and the Hulk.

Beyond the Big Top

The **acts** are death-defying. The music is delightful. The peanuts are delicious! These are only three reasons why the circus remains a beloved form of entertainment.

Circus in print

People have written stories about the circus for all ages. A 2000 novel by Darren Shan called *Cirque du Freak* is about vampires and a circus out of a nightmare. In the *Batman* series of comics and movies, Batman's partner, Robin, was born into a family of circus **aerialists** called the Flying Graysons.

Circus on screen

The animated movie *Dumbo* (1941) is about a lovable circus elephant able to do something Jumbo never could: use his big ears to fly. In 1953 the Academy Award for Best Picture went to *The Greatest Show on Earth*. The movie takes place at a Ringling Bros. and Barnum & Bailey Circus and features many real performers.

Dumbo is one circus star who continues to entertain decades after his debut.

Circus in song

The circus has inspired much music. The 1867 song "The Daring Young Man on the Flying **Trapeze**" is about Jules Léotard (see page 12). Ever since the 1950s in the United Kingdom, the song "Nellie the Elephant" has enchanted kids.

The circus is everywhere

In popular culture, clowns often appear outside the circus. Bozo the Clown shot to fame on television in the 1950s. The clown Ronald McDonald is the mascot of the McDonald's fast food chain.

The common phrase "run away and join the circus" suggests that the circus may just be the most fun place one can imagine. Many kids *do* want to run to the circus—but usually simply to watch it!

Bozo, an auguste clown, has been portrayed by hundreds of performers.

One more circus

The word "circus" also describes an out-of-control situation. At a loud, crowded store, you might say, "It's a circus in here."

Glossary

acrobat person who entertains people by performing physical feats that require a lot of strength and skill

acrobatic describes a gymnastic feat that requires a lot of skill and strength

act circus performance

advertise to announce an upcoming performance to try to interest people in coming

aerial describes something in the air

aerialist person who performs feats in the air, such as a trapeze artist

attraction interesting performance or display at a circus

comic relief something that provides humor

contortionist person who bends his or her body into extreme positions to entertain others

curiosity something a person wants to learn more about

equestrian describes horseback riding

extravaganza wonderful entertainment event

menagerie group of wild animals on display

publicity action taken to tell people about something that is for sale

ring circular area in which a circus act performs

sideshow smaller attraction at a circus

slapstick physical humor such as falling, chasing something, or bumping into something

spectator person who watches a performance

stilt special pole that performers walk on, making them appear taller

theme idea that a story is about

trapeze bar hung between two ropes and used in aerial circus acts

troupe group of performers

vertical up and down

Find Out More

Books

Cummins, Julia. *Women Daredevils: Thrills, Chills, and Frills.* New York: Dutton Children's Books, 2008.

Fleming, Candace. *The Great and Only Barnum: The Tremendous, Stupendous Life of Showman P. T. Barnum.* New York: Schwartz & Wade, 2009.

Zimmer, Tracie Vaughn. *The Floating Circus.* New York: Bloomsbury, 2008.

Websites

Circus World
http://circusworld.wisconsinhistory.org
This website by the Wisconsin Historical Society includes a photo gallery of the world's largest circus-wagon collection.

Circus Historical Society
www.circushistory.org
This website includes old photos, logos, and even a quiz.

Places to visit

Circus World Museum
550 Water Street
Baraboo, WI 53913
http://circusworld.wisconsinhistory.org/Visit/LocationDirections.aspx

The Circus Museum
5401 Bay Shore Road
Sarasota, FL 34242
www.ringling.org/circusmuseums.aspx

Index